W9-BBU-490

 CREEPY CRAWLERS IN ACTION: AUGMENTED REALITY 

PRAYING MANTISES

AN AUGMENTED REALITY EXPERIENCE

SANDRA MARKLE

Lerner Publications ◆ Minneapolis

EXPLORE INSECTS AND ARACHNIDS IN BRAND-NEW WAYS WITH AUGMENTED REALITY!

1. Ask a parent or guardian for permission to download the free Lerner AR app on your digital device by going to the App Store or Google Play. When you launch the app, choose the Creepy Crawlers in Action series.

2. As you read, look for this icon throughout the book. It means there is an augmented reality experience on that page!

3. Use the Lerner AR app to scan the picture near the icon.

4. Watch insects and arachnids come alive with augmented reality!

TABLE OF CONTENTS

A Praying Mantis's World 4

Outside and Inside 6

Hatching Nymphs 10

Adult Appetites 18

Defenses against Enemies 22

More about Praying Mantises 26

Helpful or Harmful? 26

Other Insect Heroes 27

Praying Mantis Activity 28

Glossary 29

Learn More 30

Index 31

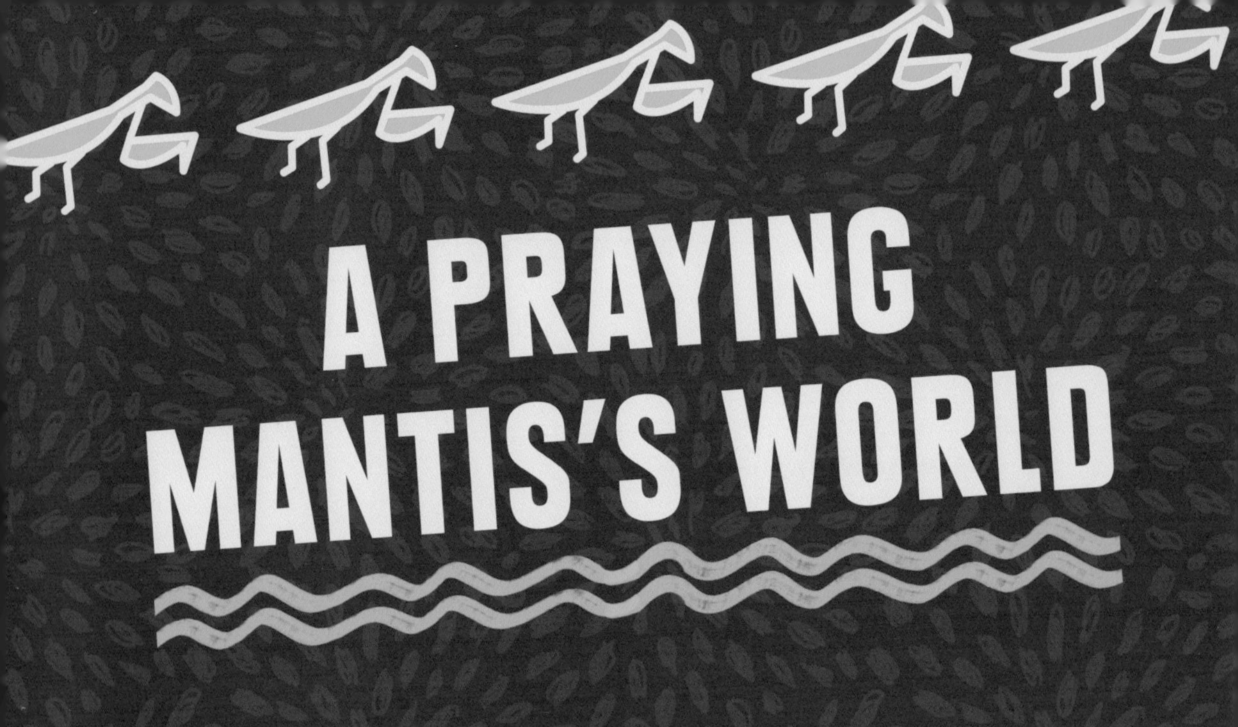

A PRAYING MANTIS'S WORLD

Welcome to the world of praying mantises. These super hunters are just one of more than a million different kinds of insects in the world. Insects live everywhere on Earth, even on the frozen continent of Antarctica.

A European praying mantis (*left*) hunts a smaller insect.

Praying mantises belong to a group of animals called arthropods (AR-throh-podz). All arthropods have segmented bodies, jointed legs, and stiff exoskeletons. Exoskeletons are skeletons on the outside like suits of armor. One way to identify an insect is to count its legs. All adult insects have six legs. They're the only animals in the world with six legs.

adult praying mantis

An adult praying mantis has six legs and three main body parts: head, thorax, and abdomen.

OUTSIDE AND INSIDE

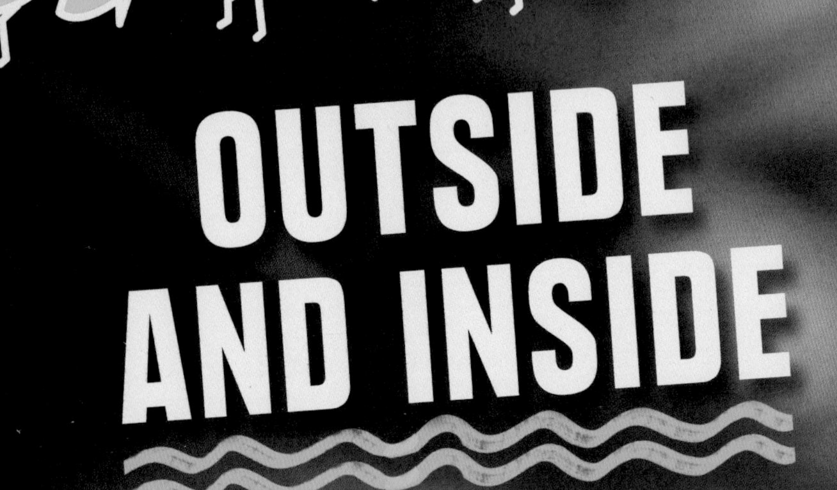

WINGS:
mantises have two pairs of wings for flight. Some female mantises have very short wings or are wingless.

ON THE OUTSIDE

If you could touch a praying mantis, its body would feel like tough plastic. The insect's exoskeleton is made up of separate plates connected by stretchy tissue that lets it bend and move. Look at this female praying mantis to discover other key features.

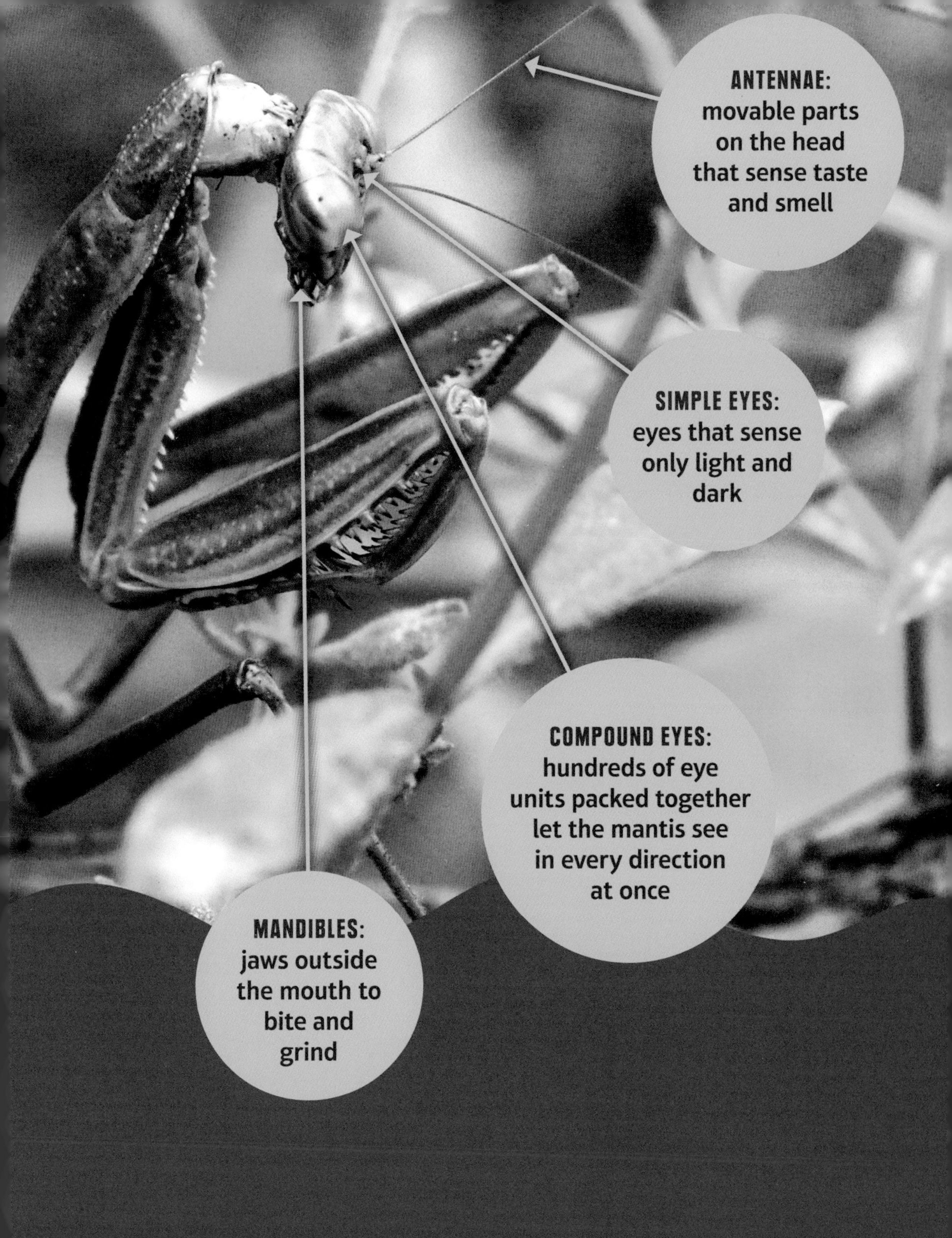
ANTENNAE: movable parts on the head that sense taste and smell
SIMPLE EYES: eyes that sense only light and dark
COMPOUND EYES: hundreds of eye units packed together let the mantis see in every direction at once
MANDIBLES: jaws outside the mouth to bite and grind

ON THE INSIDE

Look inside an adult female praying mantis.

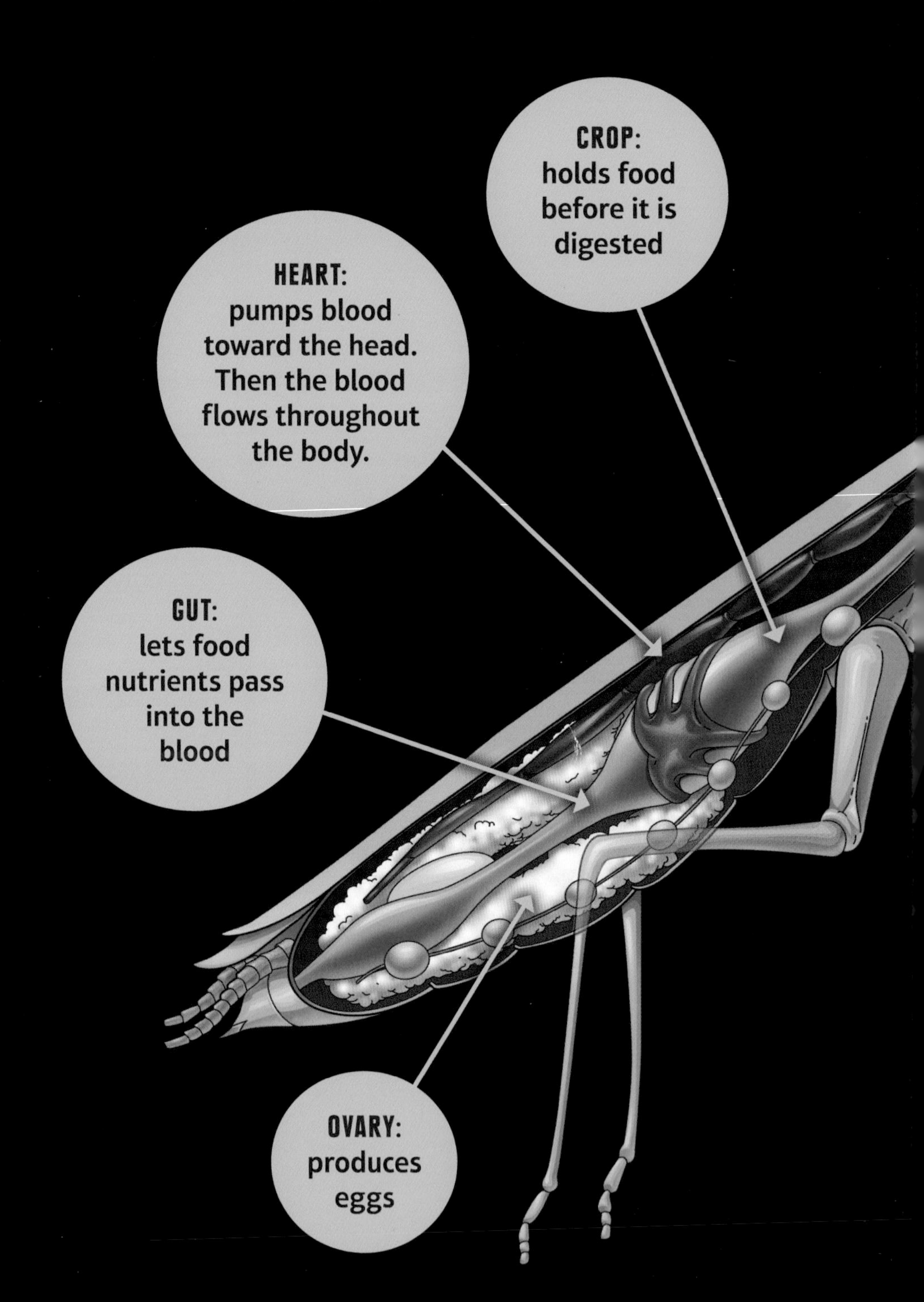

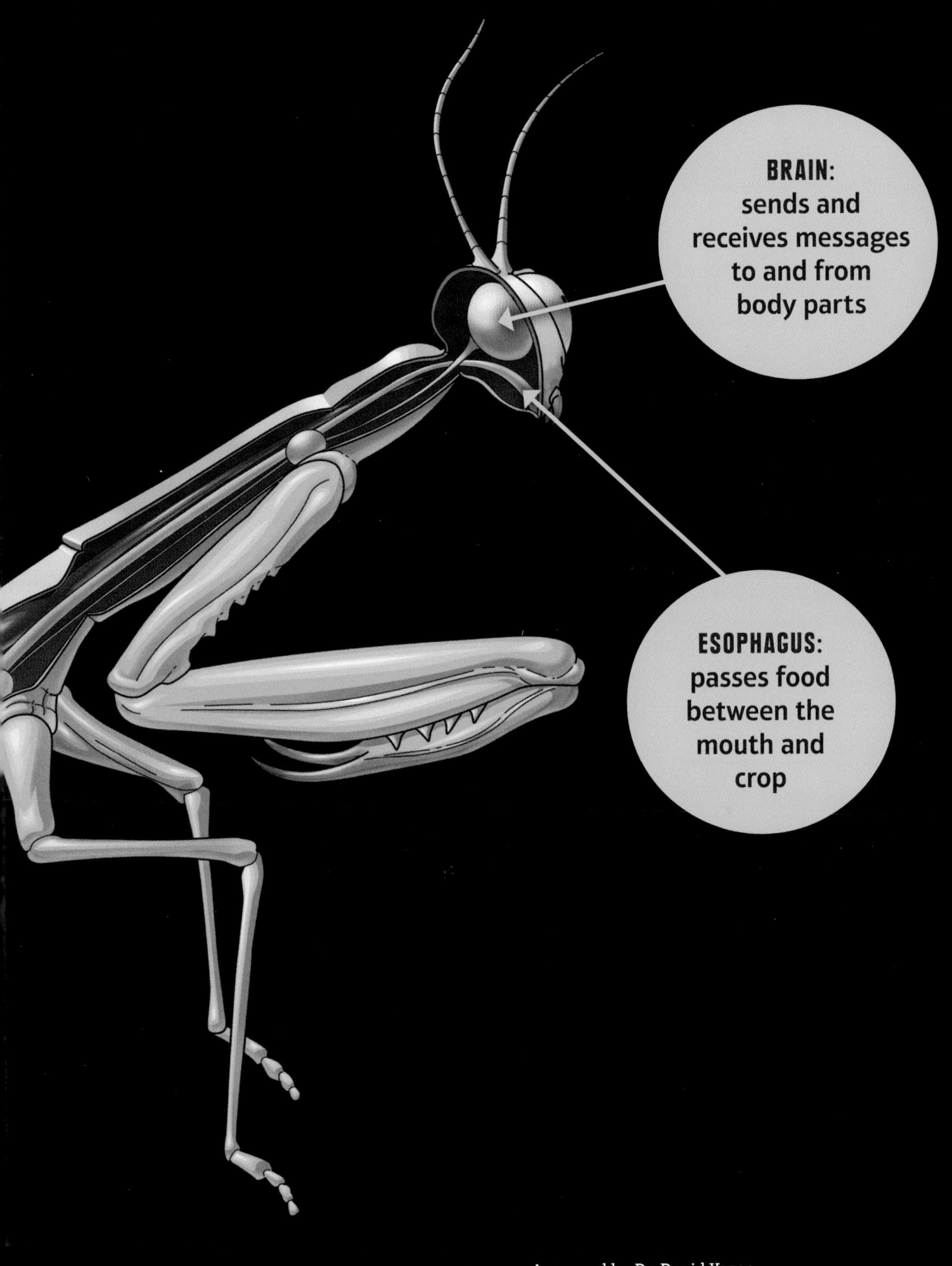

Approved by Dr. David Yager,
University of Maryland

HATCHING NYMPHS

A praying mantis uses its front legs to catch and hold prey.

Praying mantises go through three life stages: egg, nymph, and adult. The nymphs look and act much like small adults. But nymphs can't reproduce, and they can't fly until they become adults.

The focus of a praying mantis's life is hunting. As an ambush hunter, it hides and waits for prey to come close. Its body is colored to blend in with plants. It has big eyes to watch for prey.

Once its prey is near, the mantis's front legs unfold in a flash. *Snap!* It grabs its prey and bites with sharp mandibles to make the kill.

It's spring and the weather is warming up. On one tree, a European praying mantis egg case clings to a branch. All winter long, this hard, sturdy case kept the eggs inside it safe. It sheltered them from wind and rain. And it kept out egg-eating enemies, such as spiders and ants. Now nearly three hundred praying mantis nymphs are hatching. One after the other, the mantis nymphs wiggle to the egg case's opening and escape.

These praying mantis nymphs are only about 0.15 inches (0.4 cm) long. That's the same length as an eyelash on your lower eyelid.

Praying mantis nymphs are so small that many predators don't notice them.

The nymphs have an exoskeleton. It was soft while the nymphs were inside their eggs. While they wait for their exoskeletons to harden, they line up along the branch and stay close together. In a big group, each little mantis is safer from predators such as birds and spiders.

One female European mantis nymph crawls into a space among the leaves. Here, she stays hidden from predators. She is also hidden from insect prey. Her big eyes watch for anything that moves. When she spots a flying insect, she tracks it until it comes close. Her front legs unfold with lightning speed. The mantis has spines on her front legs. She drives the spines into her prey to hold on tight. She snags her first meal.

When a praying mantis attacks, its forelegs unfold and strike in a flash.

The European mantis nymph continues to hunt and eat. Soon she grows too big for her exoskeleton. She hangs upside down and molts. When she sheds her armorlike covering, she already has a new protective coat underneath. This new coat is soft at first, so she waits for it to harden. Then she starts hunting again.

Day after day, the female nymph sits on branches, waiting to ambush prey. Her shape and coloring camouflage her, or let her blend in perfectly with her surroundings.

A praying mantis molts seven to nine times before becoming an adult.

After several more molts, the European praying mantis nymph is larger and easier for predators to see. She adds to her disguise. The nymph clings to a branch with her claw-tipped feet and sways her body. This way, she blends in with the windblown leaves and twigs around her. Since she is bigger, she is able to catch bigger prey, such as caterpillars.

A European praying mantis nymph blends in with the plants where it hunts.

Later, she catches a cricket. The praying mantis kills her prey by eating it. Holding the cricket with her two front legs, the female nymph bites off a chunk. Then she bites off more. Catching one cricket after another, she feeds herself and helps keep the cricket population under control.

Praying mantises hunt by blending in with plants and waiting for prey to come near.

An orchid mantis with its wings extended

The European mantis's disguise is simple compared to some other mantis disguises. The moss mantis from Guyana has flaky bumps on its exoskeleton that make it look like a moss-covered twig. The orchid mantis from the Malaysian rain forest got its name because of its body shape. It stays still and waits for prey.

ADULT APPETITES

The European praying mantis nymph keeps on eating and growing. With each molt, her wings become bigger. By the time she molts for the seventh time, she is an adult. Her ovaries are ready to make eggs to produce young. Her wings are fully developed too. She's the biggest she's ever been and able to catch even larger prey.

European praying mantises are different shades of green or brown.

A praying mantis eats a cricket. Mantises may eat as many as fifteen crickets a day.

Over the summer, her insect prey has grown bigger too. The female mantis catches large insects every chance she gets. For her, grabbing large prey means getting a bigger helping of food. But some of these prey insects, such as grasshoppers and crickets, damage growing fruits and vegetables. By eating them, the mantis helps the people who raise and eat these crops.

Between meals, the European praying mantis cleans herself. She pulls each antenna through her mouth. Then she cleans her body and her legs. By cleaning her exoskeleton, she removes bits of dirt that could scrape a hole in it. That's important because her exoskeleton keeps her soft internal organs from drying out.

A praying mantis pulls an antenna through its mouth to clean it.

Cleaning herself also helps her be a successful hunter. She wipes the gogglelike covering over her eyes. This keeps her vision sharp. Finally, she cleans her front legs, keeping the spines ready to pinch and hold her next prey.

A praying mantis's exoskeleton even covers its eyes.

DEFENSES AGAINST ENEMIES

The adult European praying mantis is larger, so it's easier for predators to spot her. Suddenly, a bird swoops down. But before the bird gets close enough to attack, the mantis rears up on her walking legs. This makes her look even bigger. She throws up her front legs in a threat display. She flutters her wings, making a hissing sound. Startled, the bird swerves and flies away. The praying mantis's defensive actions worked!

A praying mantis makes a threat display to scare off a predator.

Some people believe female praying mantises may eat their mates. But scientists report that rarely ever happens.

Adult praying mantises fly to find new places to hunt and to escape predators. Male mantises also fly to search for a mate. When the male European mantis spots a female, he lands nearby. Then he slowly walks toward her. The male and female attract each other by waving their antennae and flexing their bodies. During mating, the male transfers a packet of sperm, male reproductive cells, to the female's body. Then the male flies away. He will search for another mate. The sperm he deposited will be stored in the female's body until she's ready to lay her eggs.

When the female is ready to lay her eggs, she first makes an egg case. She presses her tail end against a tree branch and releases a glob of jellylike material. At the same time, she twists her body around and around to whip the jelly into foam. She deposits her eggs in the foam one at a time. The foam dries quickly. In a short time, it forms a case that is too hard for egg-eating predators, such as spiders, to chew through. Its brown

A praying mantis egg case may contain hundreds of eggs.

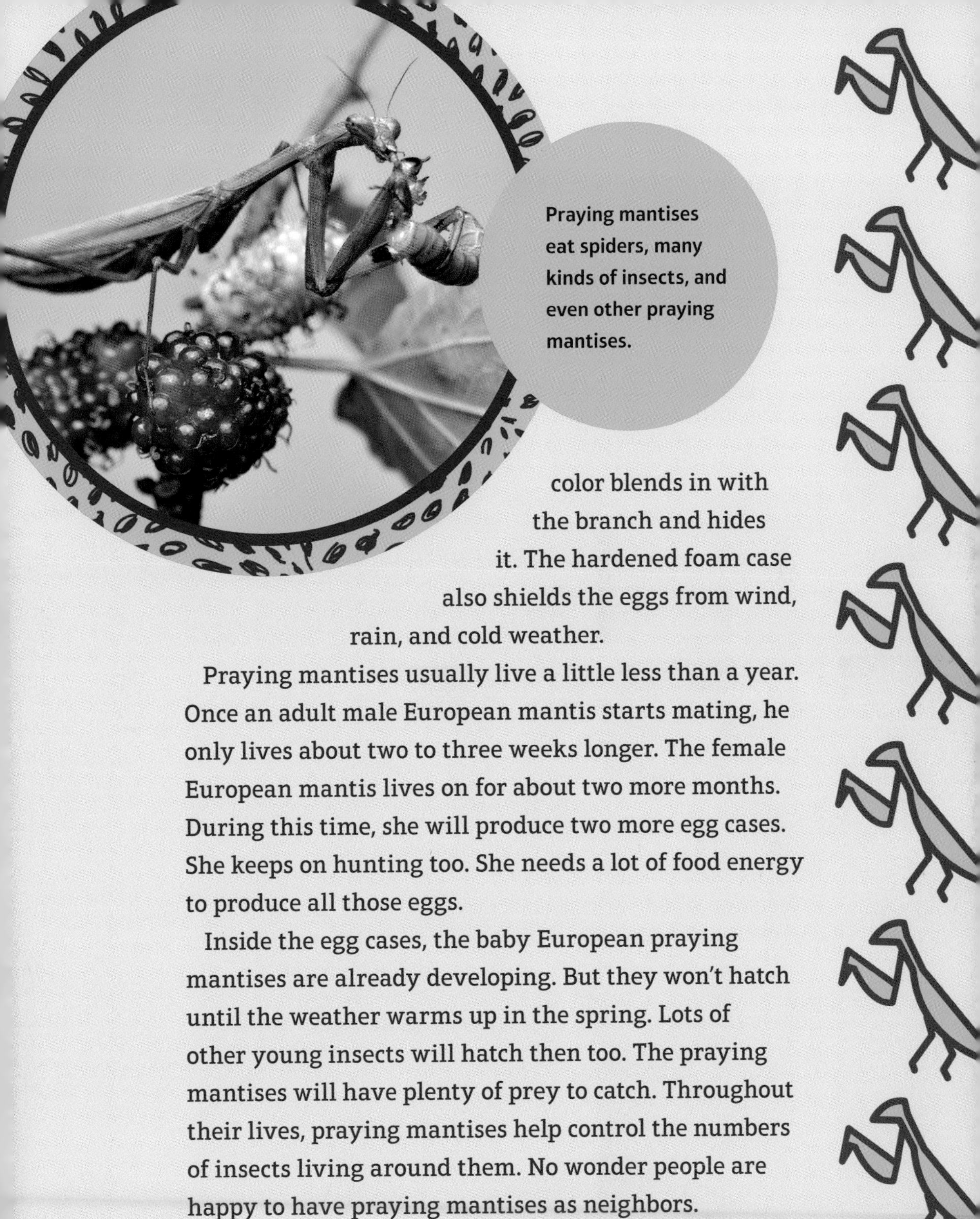

Praying mantises eat spiders, many kinds of insects, and even other praying mantises.

color blends in with the branch and hides it. The hardened foam case also shields the eggs from wind, rain, and cold weather.

Praying mantises usually live a little less than a year. Once an adult male European mantis starts mating, he only lives about two to three weeks longer. The female European mantis lives on for about two more months. During this time, she will produce two more egg cases. She keeps on hunting too. She needs a lot of food energy to produce all those eggs.

Inside the egg cases, the baby European praying mantises are already developing. But they won't hatch until the weather warms up in the spring. Lots of other young insects will hatch then too. The praying mantises will have plenty of prey to catch. Throughout their lives, praying mantises help control the numbers of insects living around them. No wonder people are happy to have praying mantises as neighbors.

MORE ABOUT PRAYING MANTISES

Praying mantises belong to a group, or order, of insects called *Dictyoptera* (dik-tee-OP-ter-ra). The name *mantis* comes from the Greek word for "prophet." The name refers to the way the insects look. Praying mantises hold their two front legs up as if in prayer. Of course, they are really getting ready to ambush prey.

Scientists group living and extinct animals with others that are similar. So praying mantises are classified this way:

kingdom: Animalia

phylum: Arthropoda (ar-throh-POH-da)

class: Insecta

order: Dictyoptera

HELPFUL OR HARMFUL?

Praying mantises are mostly helpful because they eat insects that feed on farmers' crops or garden plants. They eat any insect they can catch, though. So praying mantises sometimes also eat helpful insects, such as honeybees.

How big is a female European praying mantis? It can be up to 3 inches (7.6 cm) long.

OTHER INSECT HEROES

Other insects eat pests and are heroes too. Compare these insect hunters to praying mantises.

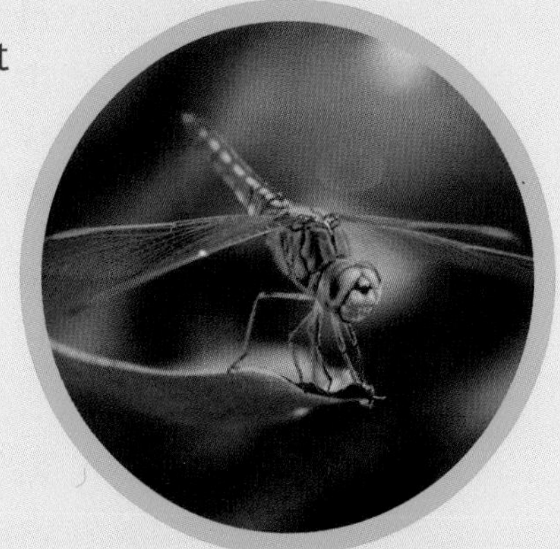

Dragonflies are winged hunters that catch insect prey in the air. They are especially valued for eating mosquitoes that might otherwise spread diseases. Dragonfly nymphs get rid of mosquitoes too. They live underwater in ponds, streams, and wetlands. They eat mosquito larvae, which also live in water.

Assassin bugs catch and kill insect prey. Like praying mantises, they hide and ambush prey. But they don't bite to kill. They stab their prey with a long beak. Digestive juices flow into the prey insect, turning its insides to liquid. Then the assassin bug sucks up its liquid meal.

PRAYING MANTIS ACTIVITY

Scientists have studied the praying mantis's strike time. That's the time from when their front legs start to move until they catch their prey. It's about seventy milliseconds—so fast it's a blur.

How fast can you react to a moving target? Work with a partner to find out. Have your partner hold a ruler by the end with the highest number. Stand beside the ruler with your hand around but not touching the lowest number. Hold your thumb on the scale side of the ruler. Have your partner release the ruler without giving you any warning. As soon as you see the ruler move, grab it. This is much like the praying mantis spotting its prey. Your reaction time is recorded in inches or centimeters—the point on the ruler closest to your thumb when you stop the ruler. The lower the number is, the faster your reaction time.

GLOSSARY

adult: the final stage of development of an insect's life cycle

egg: a female reproductive cell and the first stage of an insect's life cycle

exoskeleton: a protective, armorlike covering on the outside of the body

molt: to shed the exoskeleton

nymph: the stage between egg and adult in a praying mantis's life cycle

predator: an animal that kills and eats other animals

prey: an animal taken by another animal as food

sperm: a male reproductive cell

LEARN MORE

Borgert-Spaniol, Megan. *Praying Mantises*. Minneapolis: Bellwether Media, 2016.

Huddleston, Emma. *Beneficial Insects: Bugs Helping Plants Survive*. Minneapolis: Abdo, 2020.

Insect Facts for Kids
https://kids.kiddle.co/Insect

Johnson, Rebecca L. *Masters of Disguise: Amazing Animal Tricksters*. Minneapolis: Millbrook Press, 2016.

Mantis Facts for Kids
https://kids.kiddle.co/Mantis

Markle, Sandra. *Locusts: An Augmented Reality Experience*. Minneapolis: Lerner Publications, 2021.

Praying Mantis
https://www.ducksters.com/animals/praying_mantis.php

Praying Mantis
https://kids.nationalgeographic.com/animals/invertebrates/insects/praying-mantis/

INDEX

adult, 5, 8, 10, 18, 22–23, 25

camouflage, 14
cricket, 16, 19

egg case, 11, 24–25
eggs, 8, 10–12, 18, 23–25
European praying mantis, 11, 13–15, 17–18, 20, 22–23, 25
exoskeleton, 5–6, 12, 14, 17, 20

molt, 14–15, 18
moss mantis, 17

nymph, 10–16, 18

orchid mantis, 17

predators, 12–13, 15, 22–24
prey, 10, 13–19, 21, 25

wings, 6, 18, 22

PHOTO ACKNOWLEDGMENTS

Image credits: Cornel Constantin/Shutterstock.com, p. 4; Lutsenko_Oleksandr/Shutterstock.com, p. 5; samray/Shutterstock.com, pp. 6, 7; Bill Hauser/Independent Picture Service, pp. 8–9; iliuta goean/Shutterstock.com, p. 10; Amelia Martin/Shutterstock.com, p. 11; Guillermo Guerao Serra/Shutterstock.com, p. 12; Young Swee Ming/Shutterstock.com, p. 13; Cathy Keifer/Shutterstock.com, p. 14; Ava Peattie/Shutterstock.com, p. 15; Jesse Franks/Shutterstock.com, p. 16; Monica Anantyowati/Shutterstock.com, p. 17; Elina Litovkina/Shutterstock.com, p. 18; Detyukov Sergey/Shutterstock.com, p. 19; Marcelle Robbins/Shutterstock.com, p. 20; Joko Mardiyanto/Shutterstock.com, p. 21; serg_bimbirekov/Shutterstock.com, p. 22; I Wayan Sumatika/Shutterstock.com, p. 23; MohamedHaddad/Shutterstock.com, p. 24; Niney Azman/Shutterstock.com, pp. 25, 27 (bottom); Sagar Goswami 0901/Shutterstock.com, p. 27 (top); benevolentkira/Shutterstock.com, p. 28. Design Elements: Curly Pat/Shutterstock.com; Colorlife/Shutterstock.com. Augmented Reality experiences by Hybrid Medical Animation. Additional 3D models by Tornado Studio/TurboSquid.

Cover image: sarintra chimphoolsuk/Shutterstock.com.

The author would like to thank Dr. David Yager, University of Maryland, for sharing his expertise and enthusiasm.

Special thanks to Dr. Simon D. Pollard, University of Canterbury, Christchurch, New Zealand, for sharing his expertise and also for photo verification of the species that appear in this book.

Lerner Publications Company
An imprint of Lerner Publishing Group, Inc.
241 First Avenue North
Minneapolis, MN 55401 USA

For reading levels and more information, look up this title at www.lernerbooks.com.

Main body text set in Aptifer Slab LT Pro medium.
Typeface provided by Linotype AG.

Library of Congress Cataloging-in-Publication Data

Title: Praying mantises : an augmented reality experience / Sandra Markle.
Description: Minneapolis : Lerner Publications, [2021] | Series: Creepy crawlers in action : augmented reality | Includes bibliographical references and index. | Audience: Ages 8–12 | Audience: Grades 4–6 | Summary: "A praying mantis waits for a prey insect to appear. Then, like lightning, the mantis strikes! Learn how praying mantises hunt, reproduce, and protect themselves with thrilling details and awesome augmented reality experiences"— Provided by publisher.
Identifiers: LCCN 2020016354 (print) | LCCN 2020016355 (ebook) | ISBN 9781728402734 (library binding) | ISBN 9781728417912 (ebook)
Subjects: LCSH: Praying mantis—Juvenile literature.
Classification: LCC QL505.9.M35 M365 2021 (print) | LCC QL505.9.M35 (ebook) | DDC 595.7/27—dc23

LC record available at https://lccn.loc.gov/2020016354
LC ebook record available at https://lccn.loc.gov/2020016355

Manufactured in the United States of America
1-48259-48826-6/25/2020